California State Capitol

Sacramento

Jane Moorman

There is a saying, "It was a Friday night and it seemed like a good idea at the time." That sums up the beginning of the State Capitols Project.

When I told my brother of my idea of photographing state capitols, he said, "You do know there are 50 states and two of them you can't drive to."

Each capitol has its own unique beauty that reflects the state's personality when it was built.

Jane Moorman, photographer

California Statehouse

During the first ten years of California's statehood, its capitol was located in four cities before reaching its permanent location in Sacramento.

Construction began on the present building in 1860 and was completed in 1874. Architects Miner Frederick Butler and Reuben Clark combined Greek Revival and Roman-Corinthian architectural styles.

Exterior materials included California granite with plaster on brick and cast iron.

A series of seismic reports in the 1970s condemned the building's structural integrity.

California and its leaders confronted the stark choice to either replace the building with new structures or restore the original building.

In 1975, when the capitol restoration project began, the building's exterior decorative elements had deteriorated to the point that they posed a serious threat to the public.

Inside, during the many decades, much of the original decorations had been painted over or removed.

Restoration of the building began in 1976 and lasted six years, about half the time it took to construct the original building a century earlier.

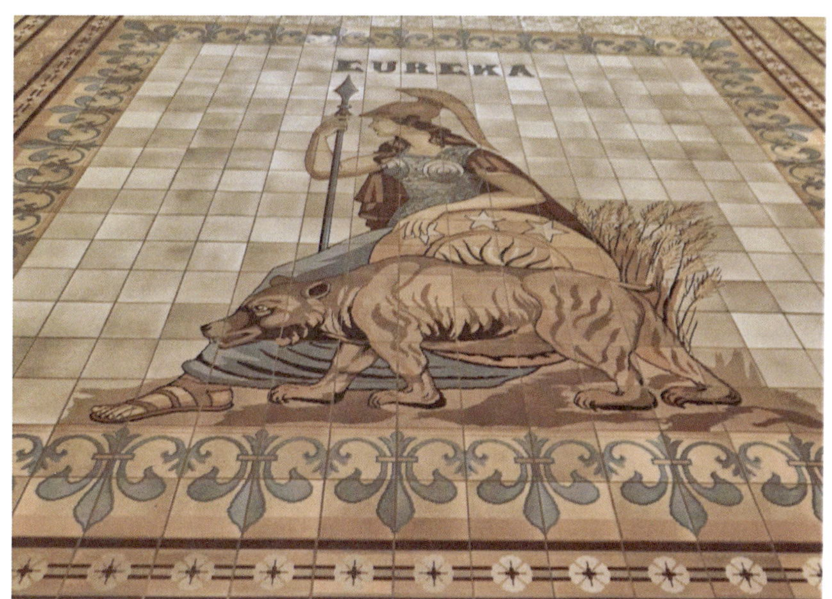

Symbolism of Minerva

A large tile grouping featuring Minerva seated with California grizzly bear and the word Eureka is located in the first floor hallway.

"Eureka" is California's state motto and translates from the original Greek to "I have found it."

According to ancient Roman myth, the goddess Minerva was born fully grown. In similar manner, California became a state without first being a territory. Minerva's image throughout the capitol symbolizes California's direct rise to statehood.

The present tile floor covering includes reproductions of tiles that were originally purchased from the Mosaic Tile Company of Zanesville, Ohio, and installed in 1896.

Golden Dome

A gold-plated copper ball, reminiscent of a gold nugget, is affixed to the cupola at the apex of the capitol's copper dome 242 feet above the ground.

The pediment on the west side of the building contains statuary created by Pietro Mezzara. In the center stands Minerva, an 11-foot-high figure dressed in classical robes, holding a lance and shield, with a bear crouched at her feet. The statues to her left symbolize Justice and Mining, those to her right, Education and Industry.

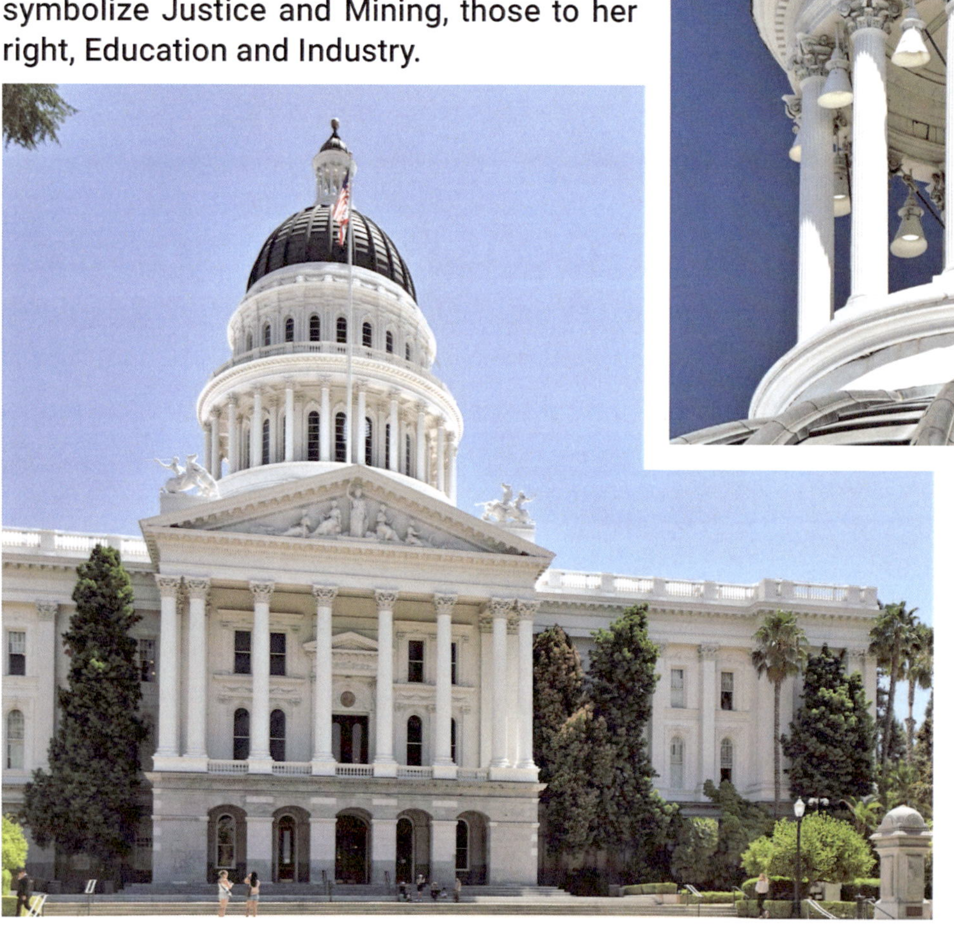

Capitol Adorned with Gold and Statuary

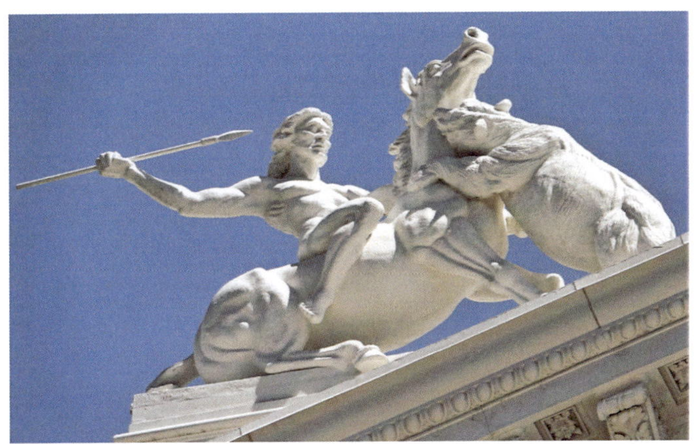

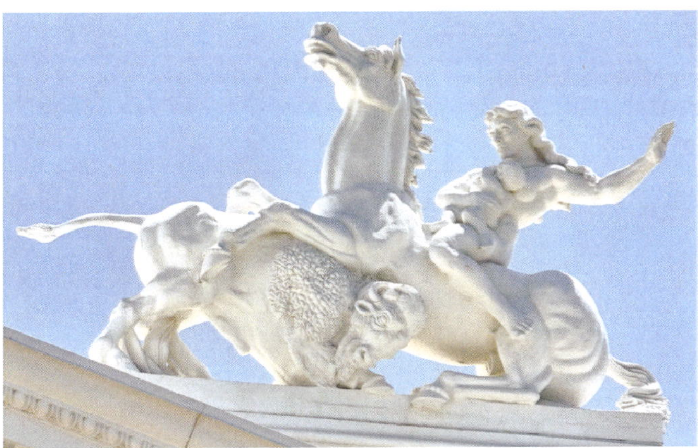

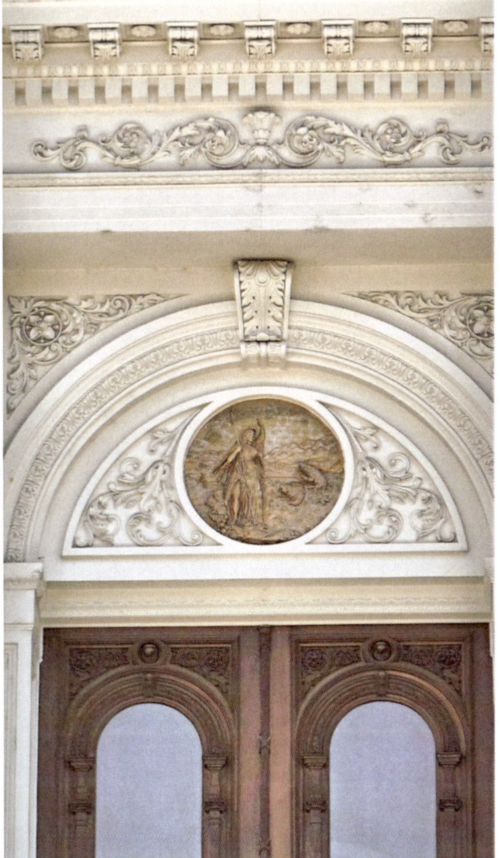

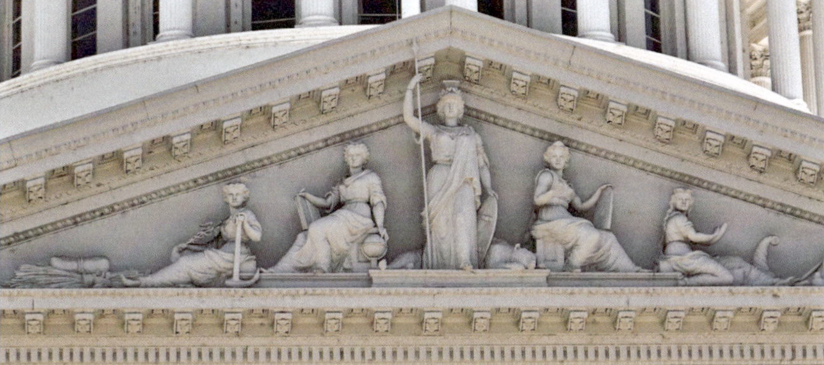

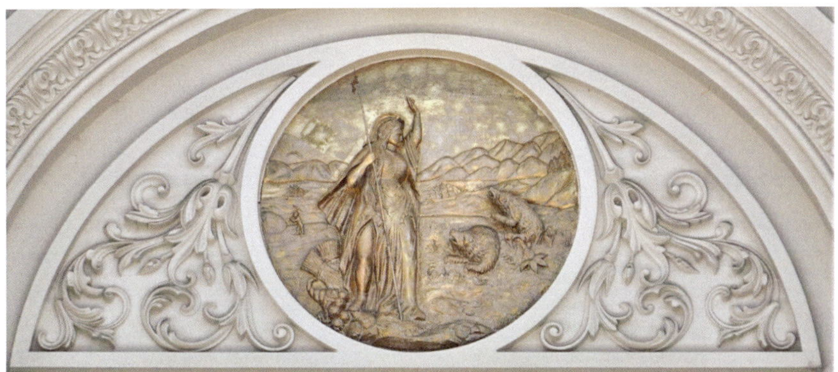

Minerva, in an early version of the state seal, greets visitors from above the grand entrance.

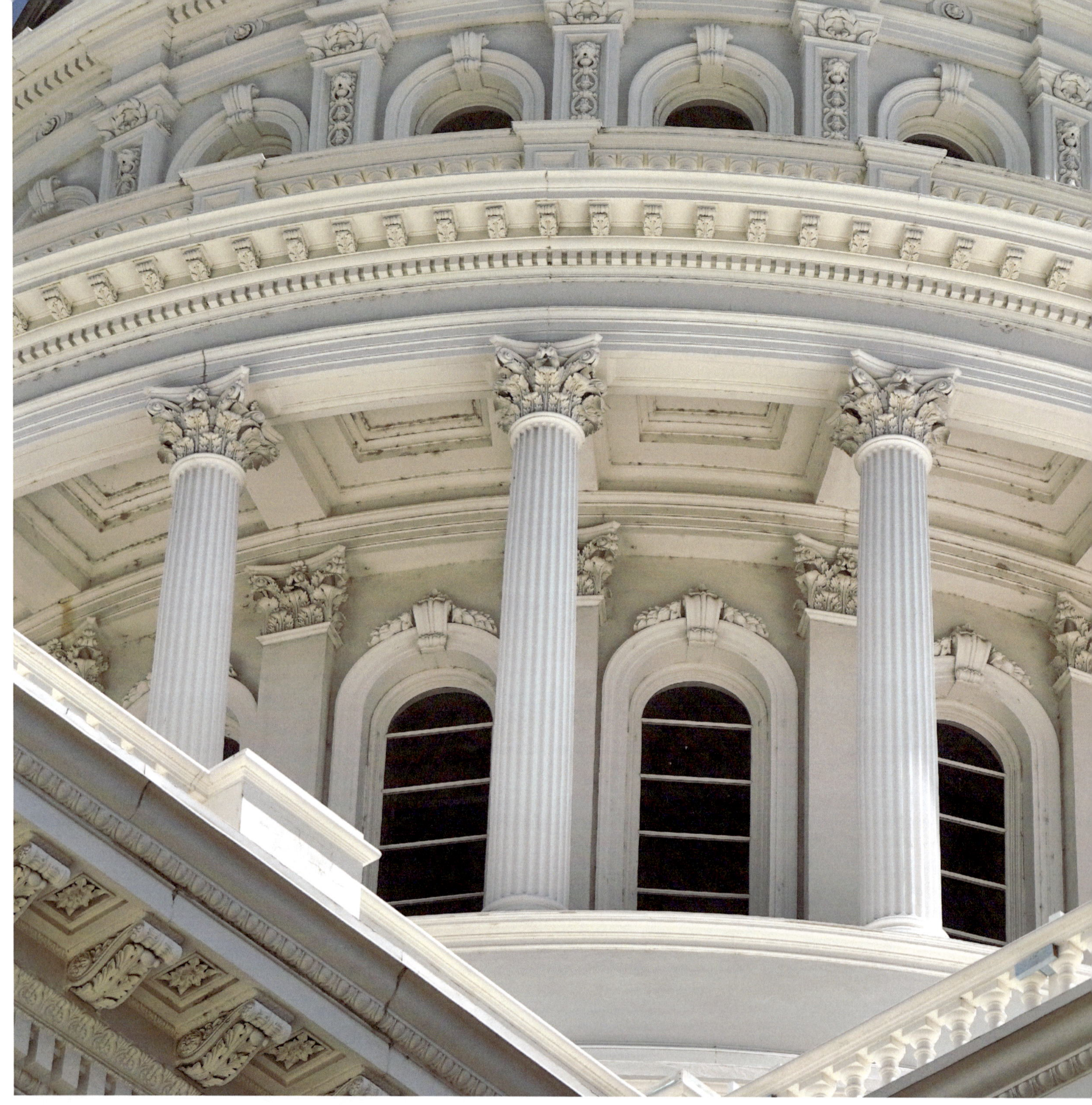

Great Seal of the State of California

The Great Seal is one of many symbols that decorate the capitol and represent the state's people and resources.

The present seal was officially adopted on Oct. 2, 1849. In 1907, a stained glass representation of the Great Seal was installed in the ceiling of the second floor hallways leading from the capitol's rotunda.

After the 1970s building restoration, the stained-glass seal welcomes visitors into the capitol museum.

Images on the seal include Minerva, a grizzly bear, a gold miner, ships, the state motto and 31 stars. Following is the symbolism of these images.

The Roman goddess of wisdom, craftsmen and warriors, Minerva was fully born as an adult. She symbolizes California's political birth as a full-fledged state without having previously been a territory.

The grizzly bear at the feet of the seated Minerva represents the oldest unofficial state symbol for California -- The Bear Flag. This majestic state animal has come to symbolize the state's remarkable wildlife. The bear feeds on grain and grapes, which presents the bountiful produce of the state's rich farmland.

The miner busy digging the earth for gold with his pick represents the extraordinary mineral wealth of California that earned its nickname - Golden State.

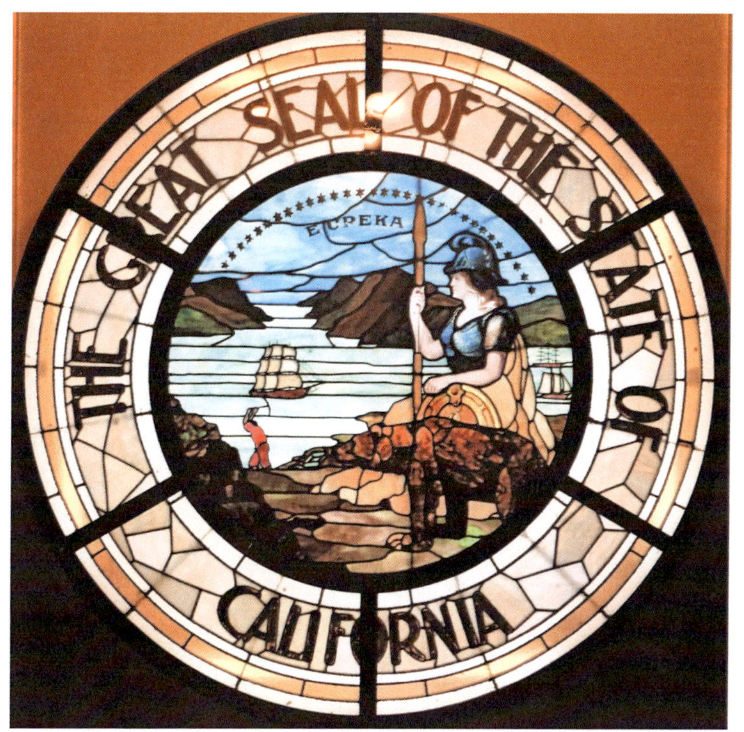

The various sailing ships and steam vessels that lay at anchor before the mighty mountains of the state symbolize the maritime trade and commercial wealth that would make California into the major economic power of today.

The state motto is Eureka, the Greek word found at the top of the seal, means "I have found it." Legend has it that the word was first uttered by an ancient Greek scientist. It is a fitting state motto because of the golden wealth that was discovered among its mountains and rivers.

The 31 stars that arch over the goddess Minerva symbolize California's entrance into the Union as the 31st state in 1850.

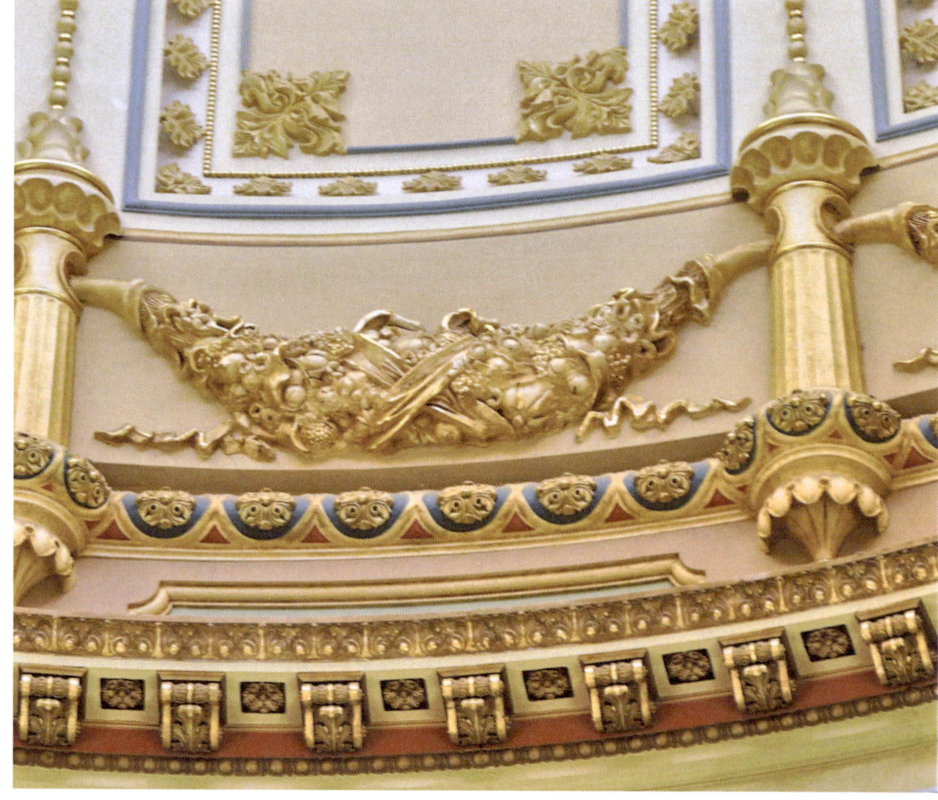
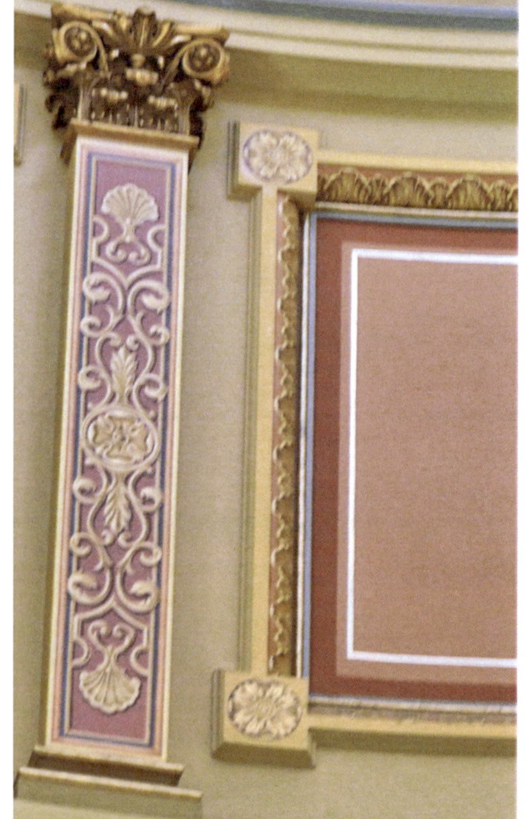

Interior Dome Reflects Renaissance Revival Style

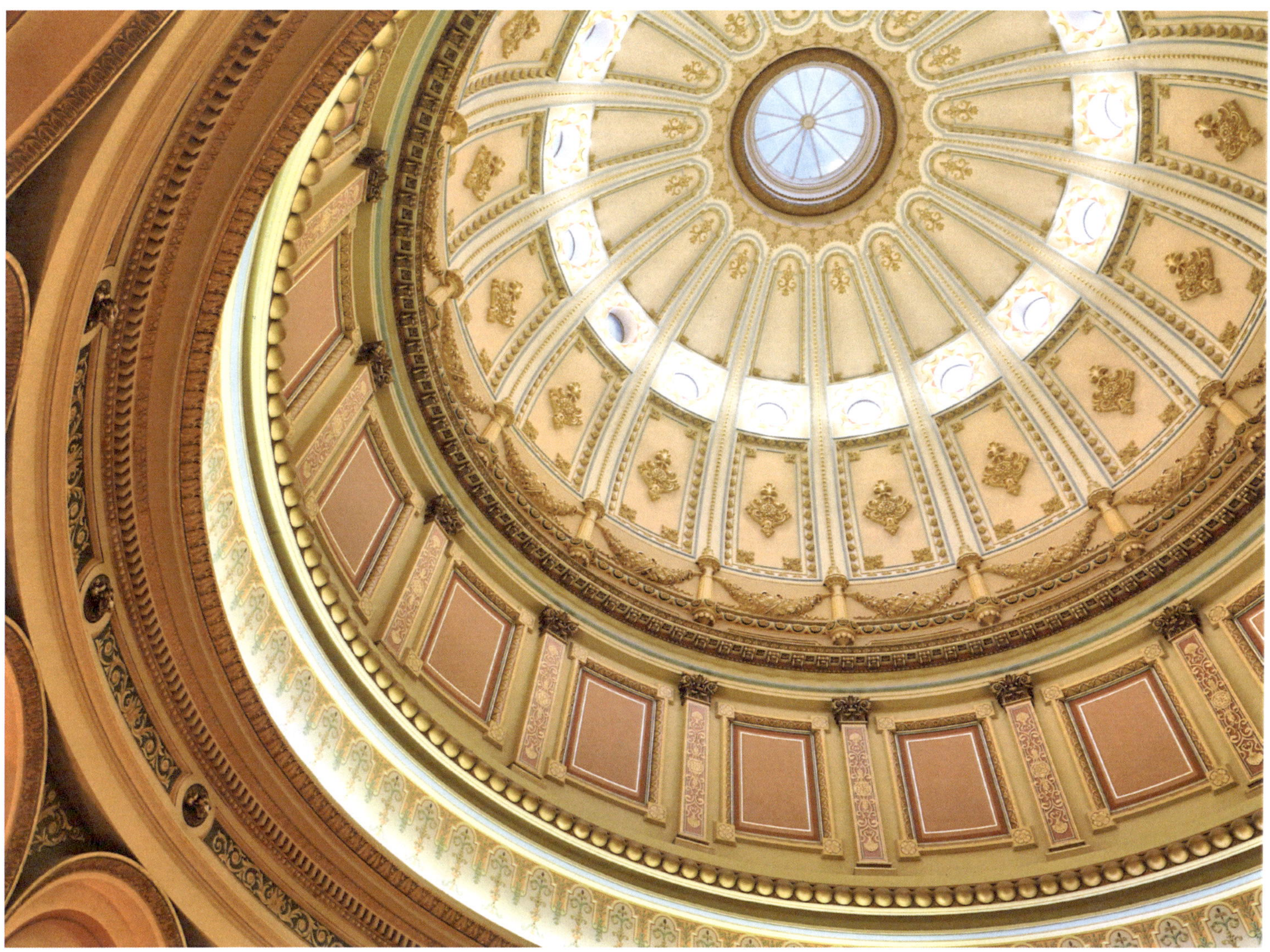

Classical renaissance elements decorate the interior of the 128-foot dome. The frescoing of the interior dome reflects the Renaissance Revival style popular during Victorian time. Fleur-de-lis patterns hand-painted in soft pastels and decorative plaster festoons adorned in gold reflect light from the dome's skylight. A band of cast iron grizzly bears look down on visitors. The skylight makes a chandelier unnecessary.

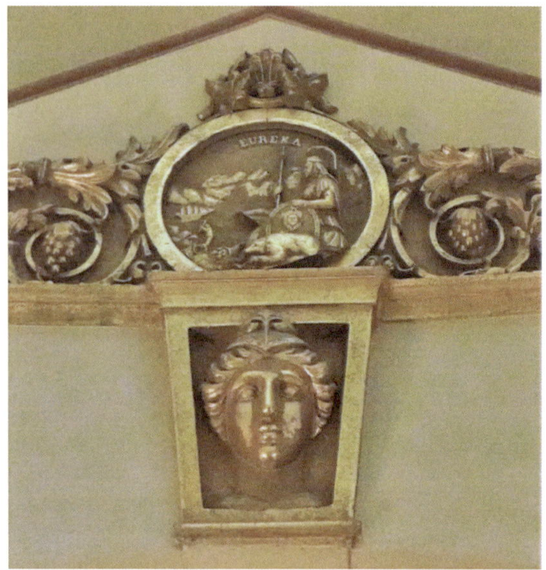

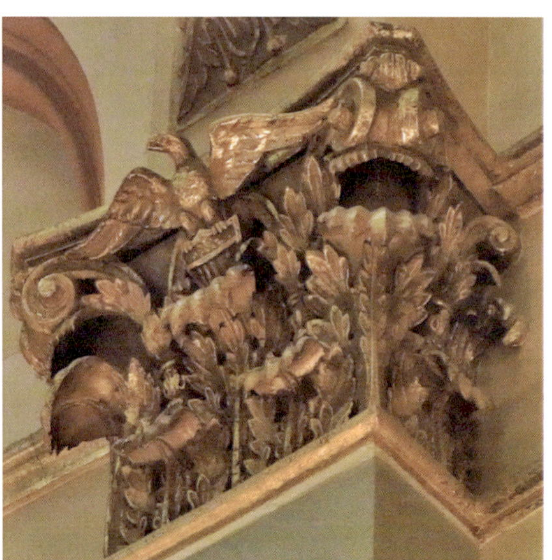

    The most impressive decorations in the rotunda are the California state symbols. Stylized versions of Minerva, the Roman goddess who is featured on the Great Seal of California, sit atop the arched openings that lead into the second-floor rotunda walkways. Majestic eagles grace the Corinthian capitals of the pilasters that surround the rotunda. Such California' specific ornamentation exists throughout the rest of the building.

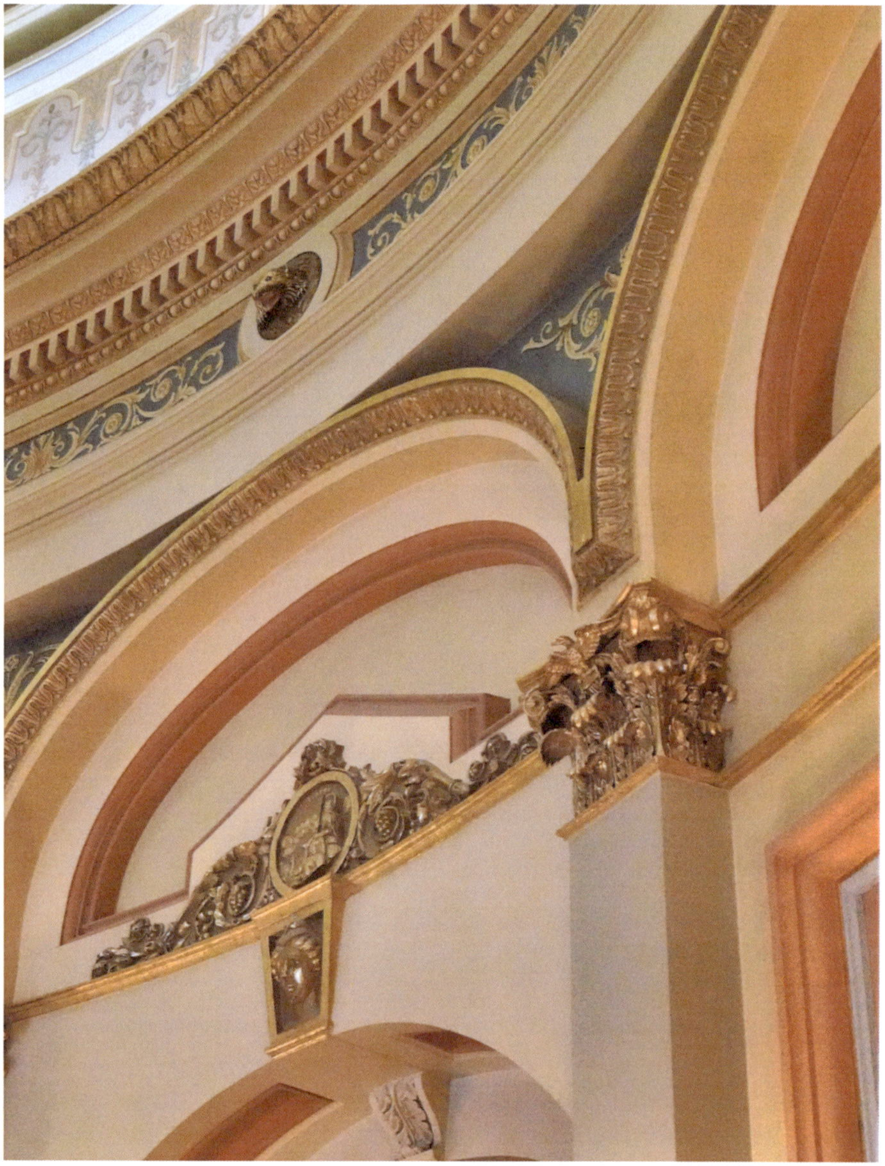

Encaustic Tiles Highlight Rotunda Second Floor

The 6,000 tiles laid in the Capitol's second floor rotunda are a geometric mosaic of earth-toned shapes, creating a "marquetry" effect similar to the inlaid woodwork in Renaissance revival style furniture. Maw and Company manufactured the original tile in Shropshire, England.

During the late 1800s, Maw and Company was one of the foremost tile manufacturers in the world. Master tile makers created each encaustic tile used for the capitol rotunda by hand. Artisans filled each indentation in the pattern with colored, liquid clay. They then added subsequent colors until the pattern was completed.

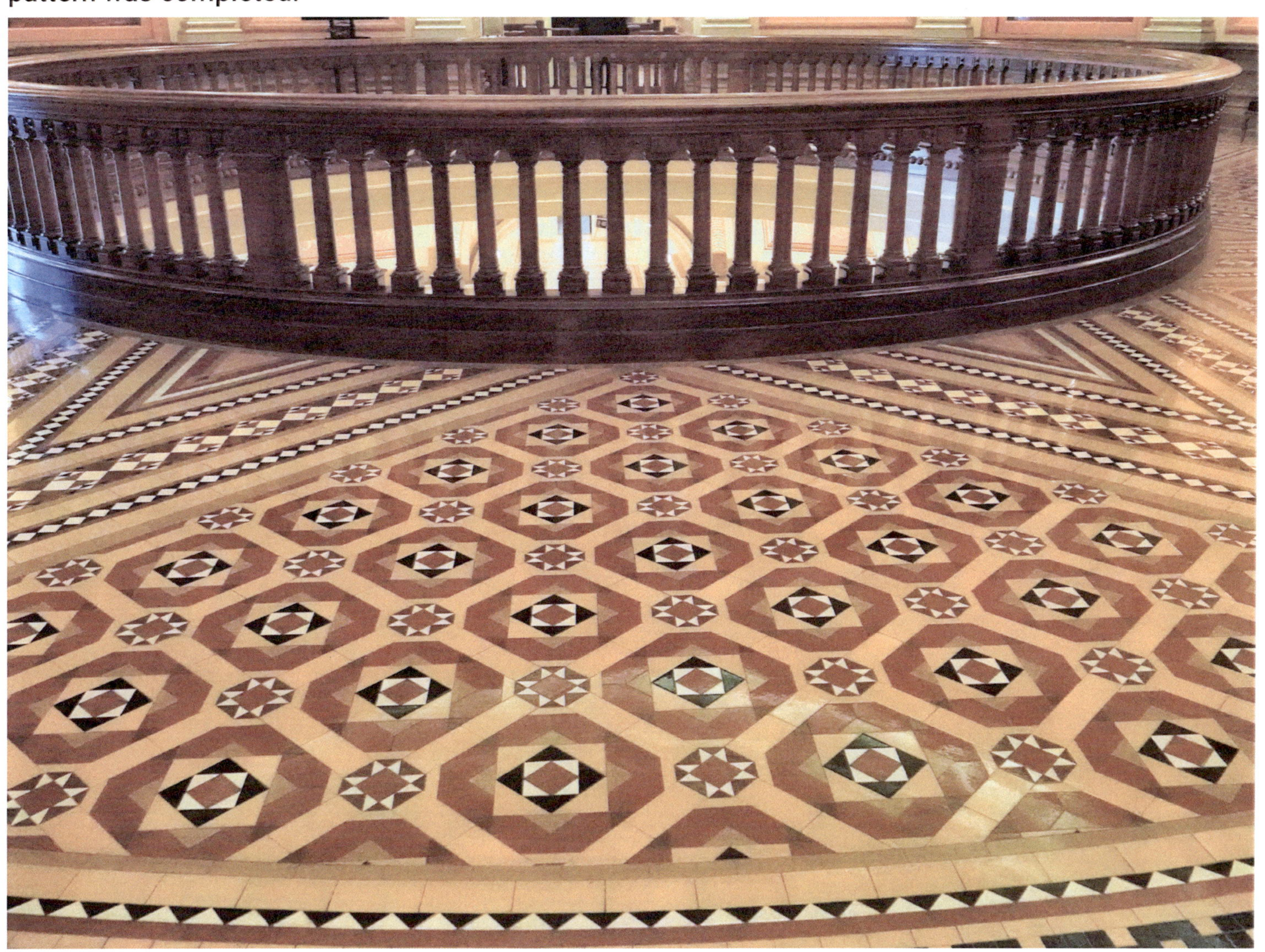

Legislative Chambers Reflect Historical Colors

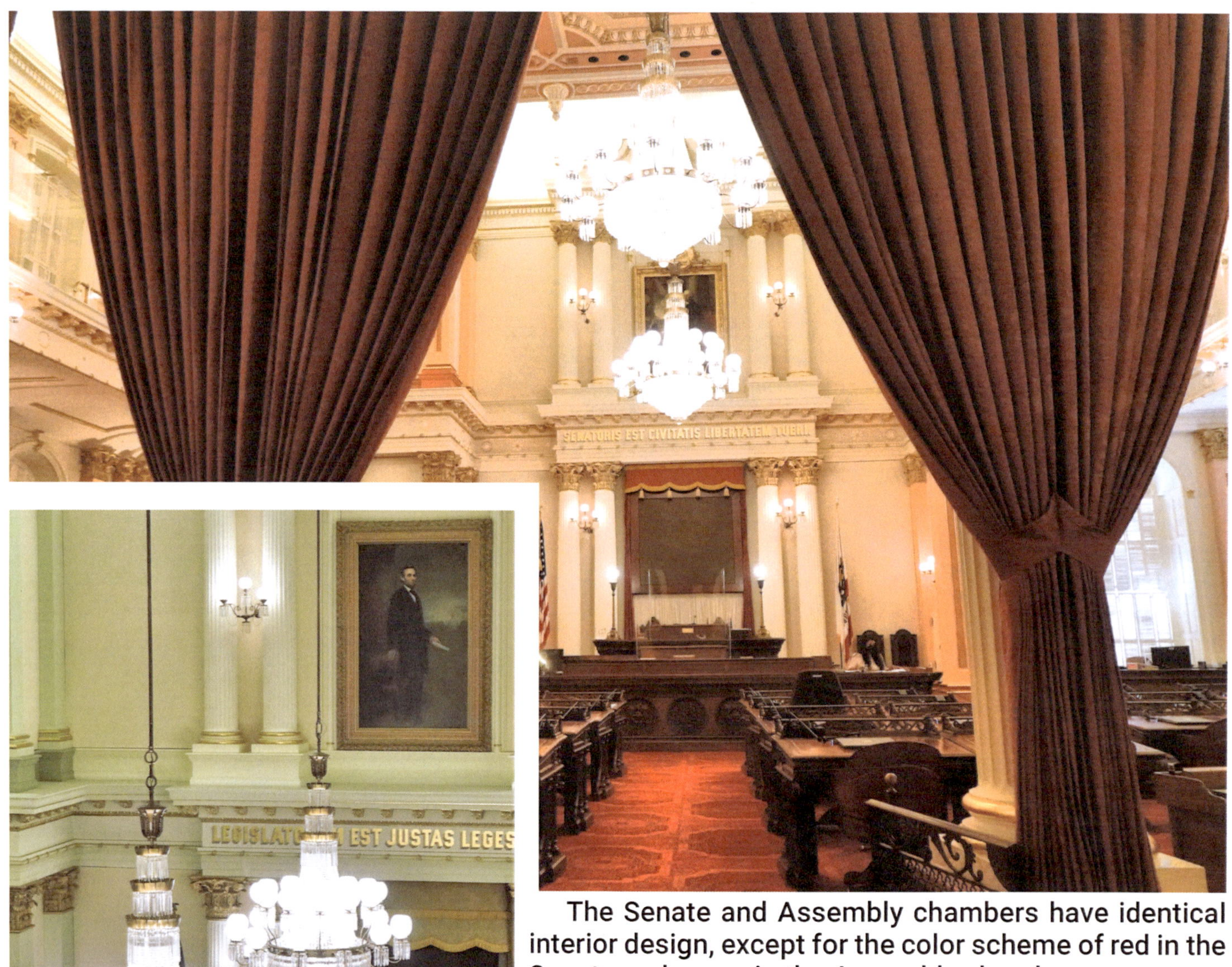

The Senate and Assembly chambers have identical interior design, except for the color scheme of red in the Senate and green in the Assembly chamber.

The colors of the chambers are traced back to the British Parliament, where red is used in the House of Lords and green is used in the House of Commons.

A portrait of George Washington is in the Senate, while a portrait of Abraham Lincoln is in the Assembly chamber.

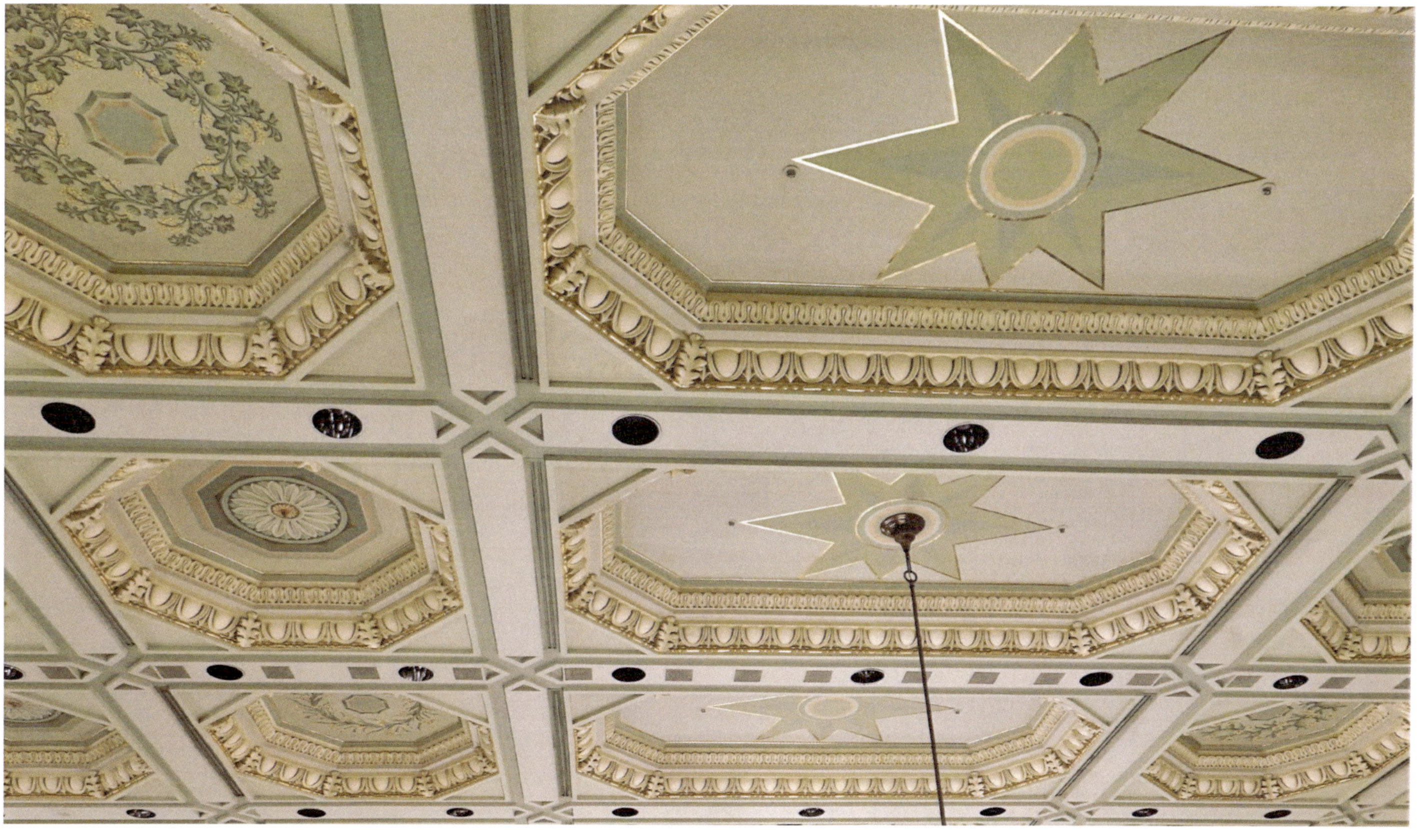

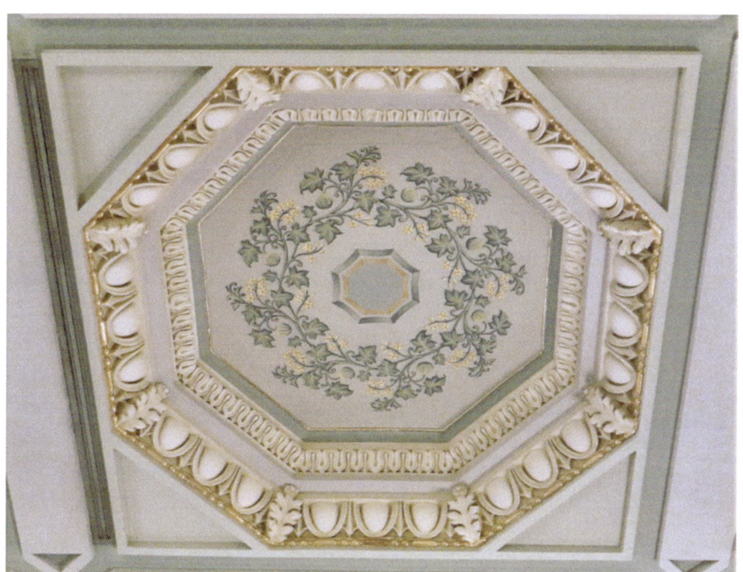

The rooms are a blend of old and new. Original desks from 1869, authentically recreated chandeliers, and decorative ceilings contrast with modern sound systems and video cameras.

The Latin motto above the dais, remindthe elected officials of their role in democracy.

Senate: "Senatoris Est Civitatis Libertatem Tueri" -- It is the duty of the Senate to protect the liberty of the citizens.

Assembly: "Legislatorum Est Justas Leges Condere" -- It is the duty of the legislators to make just laws.

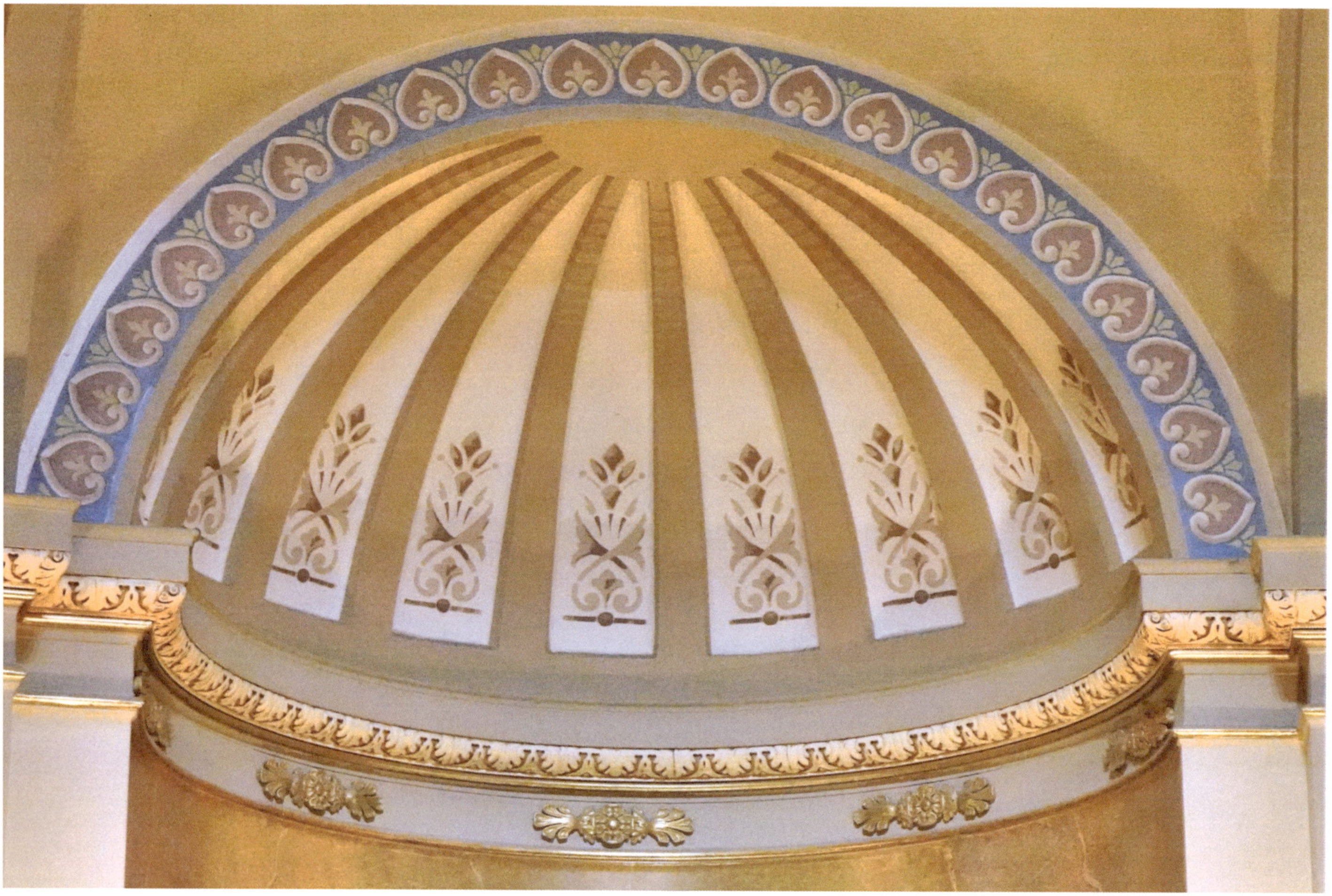

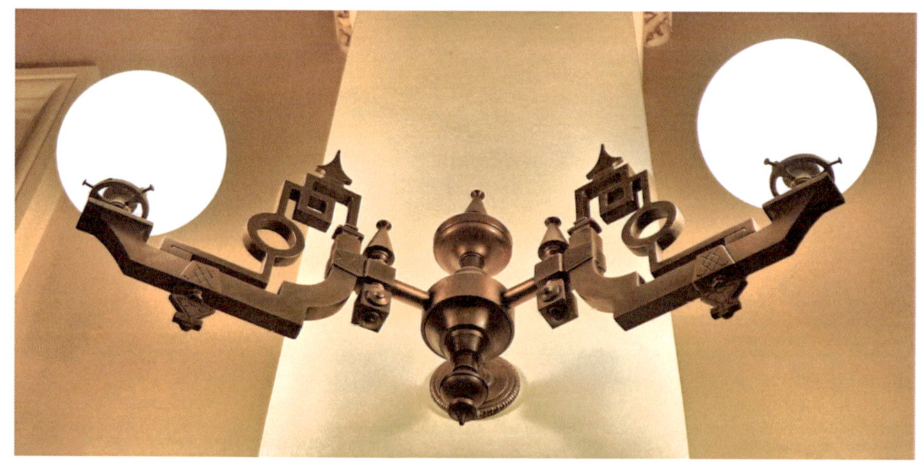

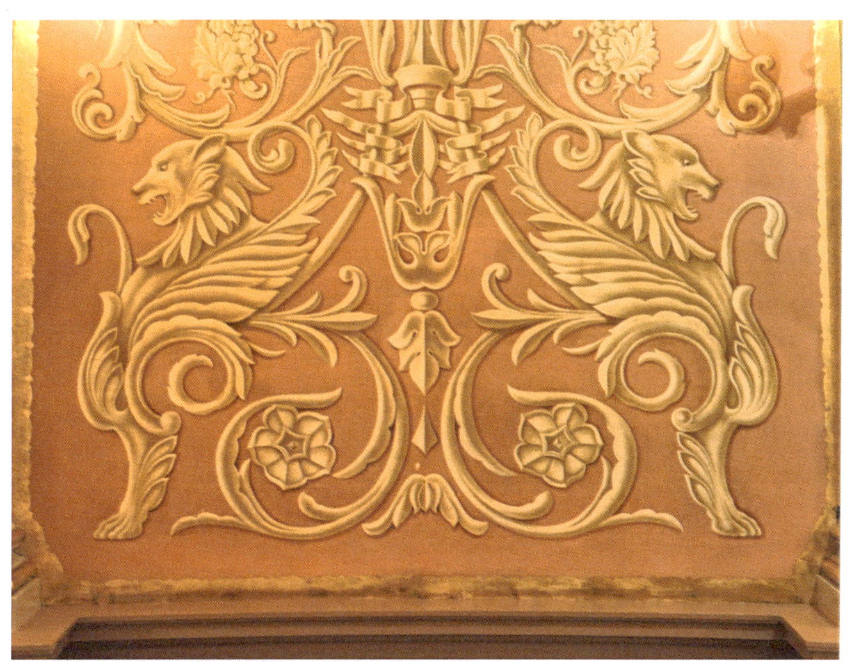

Motifs of swirling foliage, urns, and stylized griffins, a mythical animal with the head of a lion and the body of an eagle, decorate the walls.

Artists first painted the murals on canvas, after which workers permanently attached them to the plaster walls. Separating these murals are four barreled niches featuring faux marbleized paint. Inside the niche are urns, which on occasions, hold fresh-cut flower arrangements.

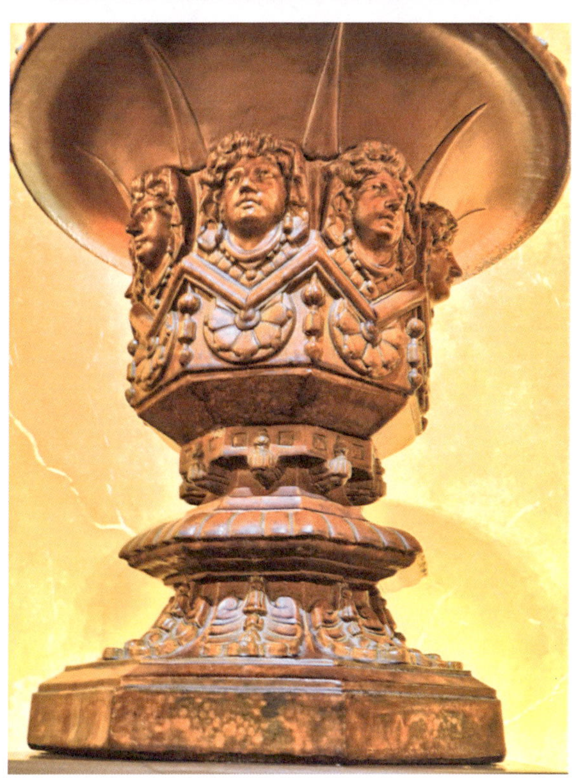

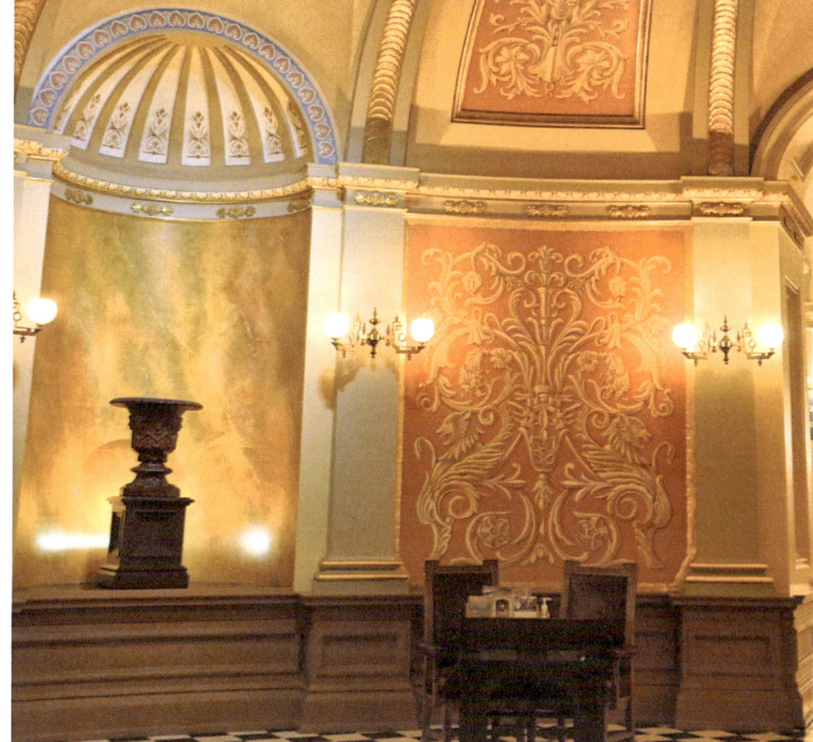

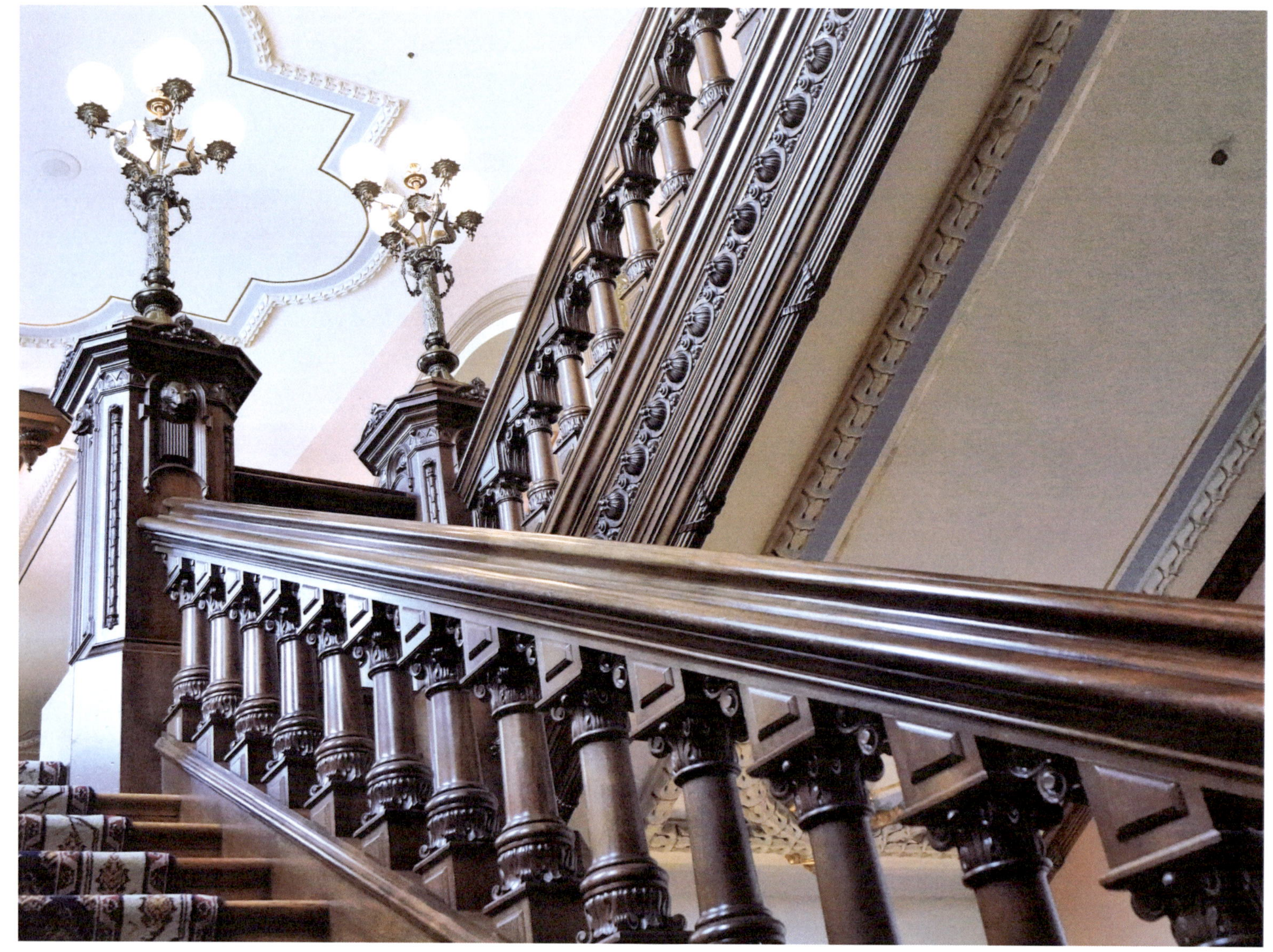

Grand Staircase Hand-carved Mahogany, Ash

The original grand staircases were removed from the capitol in 1906 to make way for additional office space and elevators. Recreating the staircases was a daunting task. The only reference was two black-and-white photographs.

Fortunately, researchers located one of the original newel posts and were able to obtain it from St. Francis of Assisi Church.

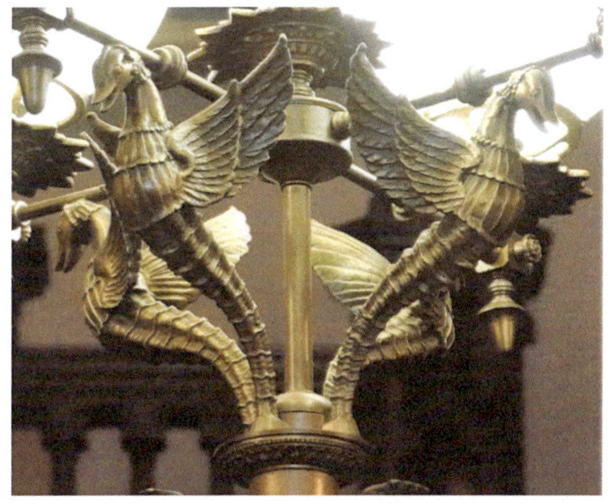

The newel posts chandeliers are copies of the original gaslights and include flying seahorse ornaments drawn from Greek mythology.

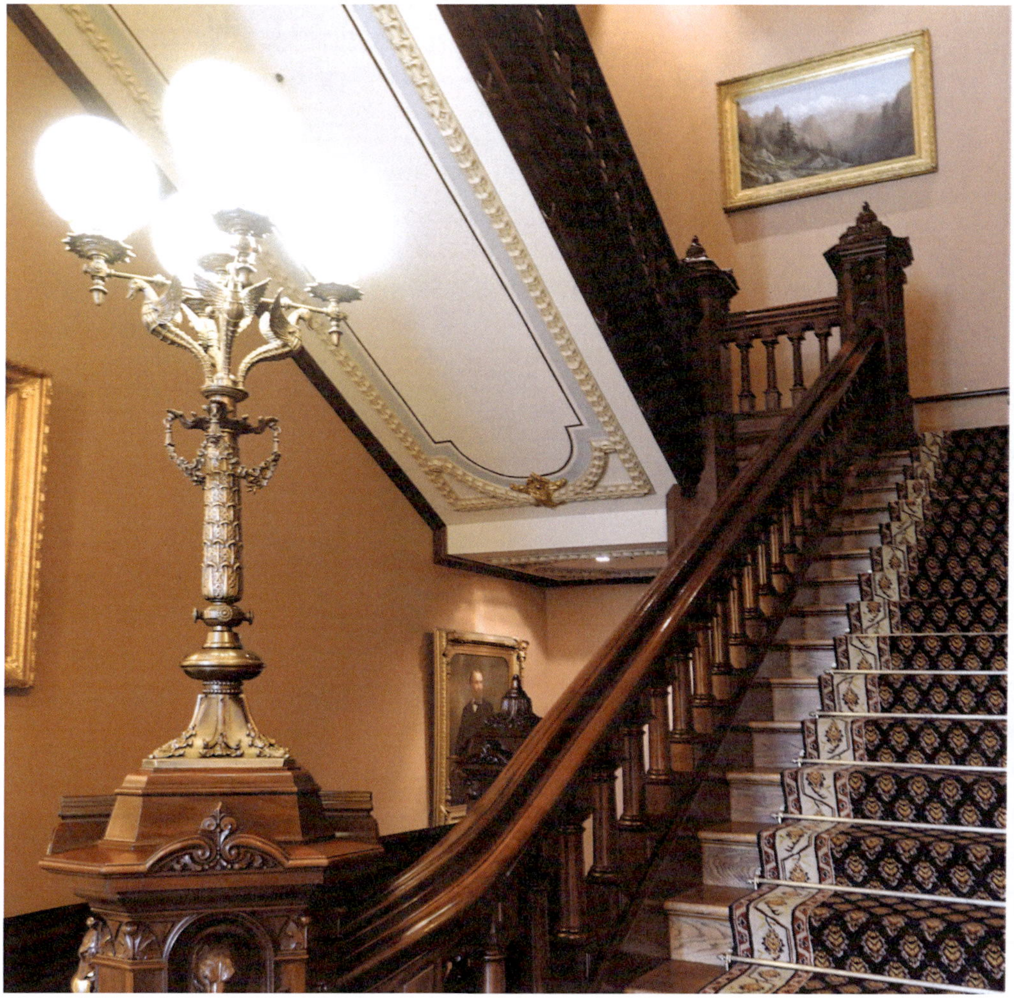

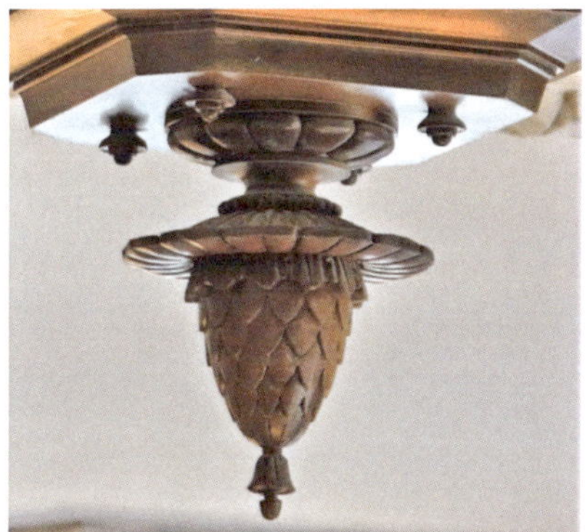

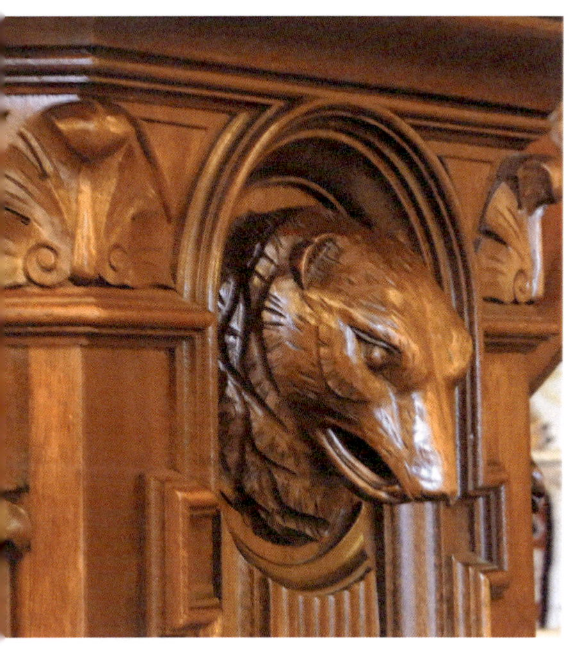

Using the original as a model, craftspeople recreated the hand-carved walnut, mahogany, and redwood posts featuring heads of a bear and foliage.

Originally, wood-carved pinecones were atop the newel on the landings. The pinecones were broken off by people pulling on them as they turned the corner of the stairs. Now the pinecones hang upside down from the ceiling of the landings.

1906 State Offices Display the Way it Was

Replicas of the historical governor an state treasurer offices from 1906 are in the first-floor museum wing. The governor's three-room suite was used by the elected official until 1951.

During the restoration of the ceilings, much of the plaster detail needed to be redone. Workers used cake decorating tubes to recreate the original texture and shade of plaster.

Parget is the colorful plaster decoratio that can be seen in the ceilings. Unique plaster designs were once common throughout the building.

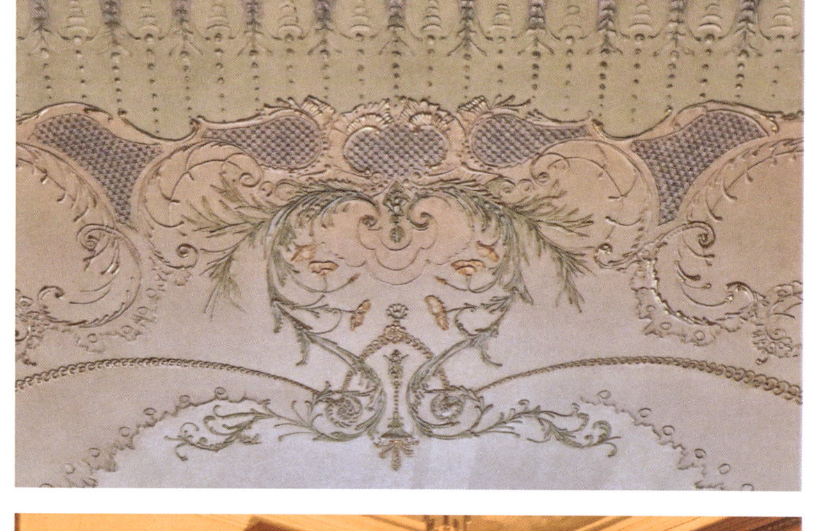

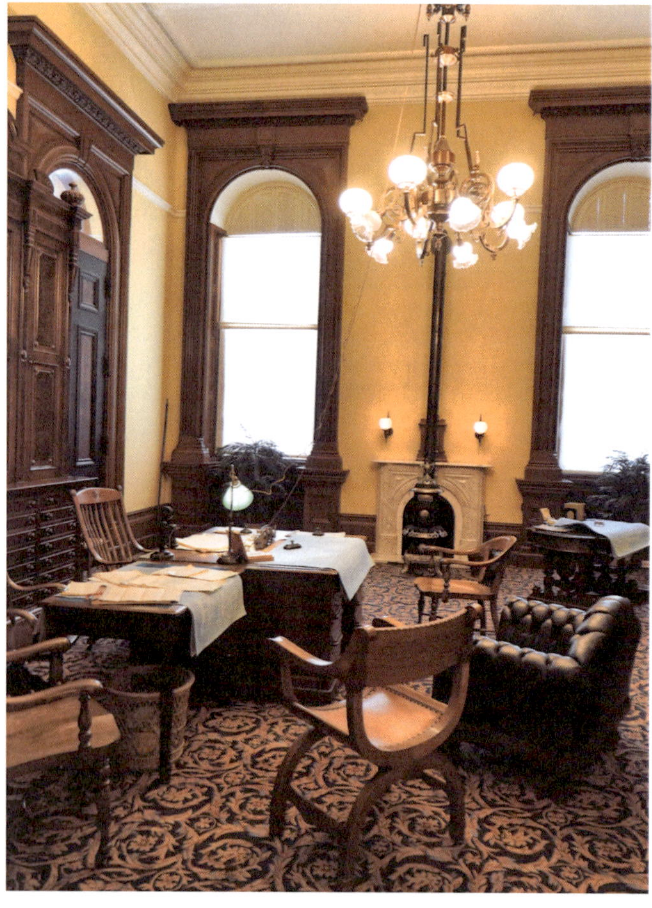

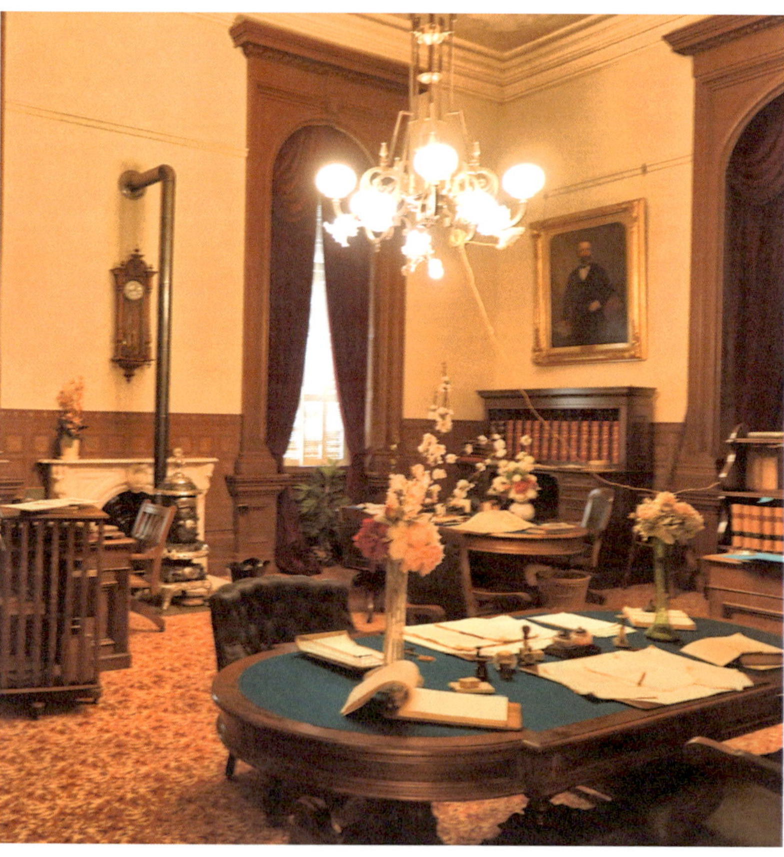

Arthur F. Mathews Murals Depict State History

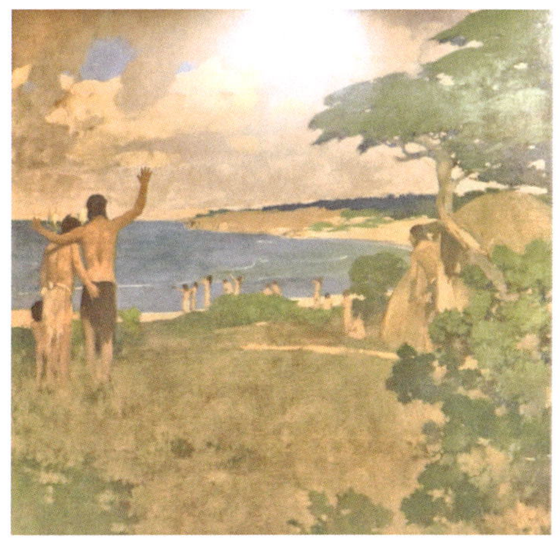
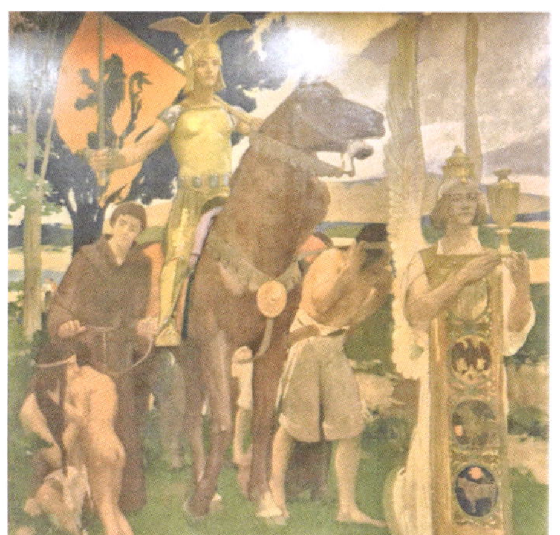
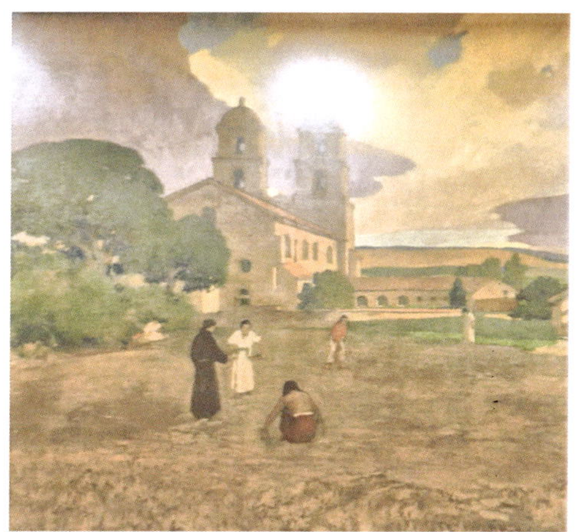
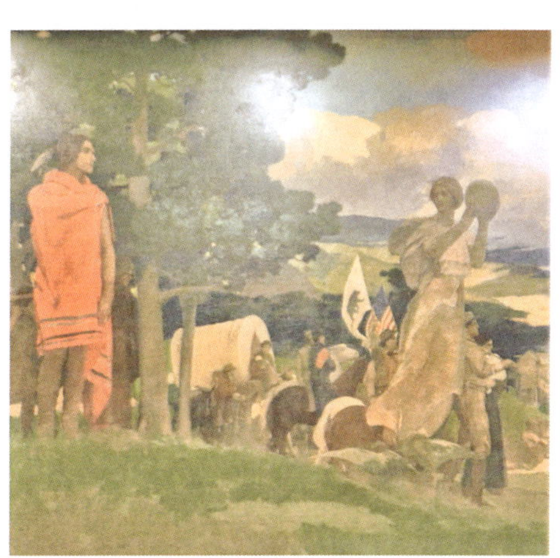
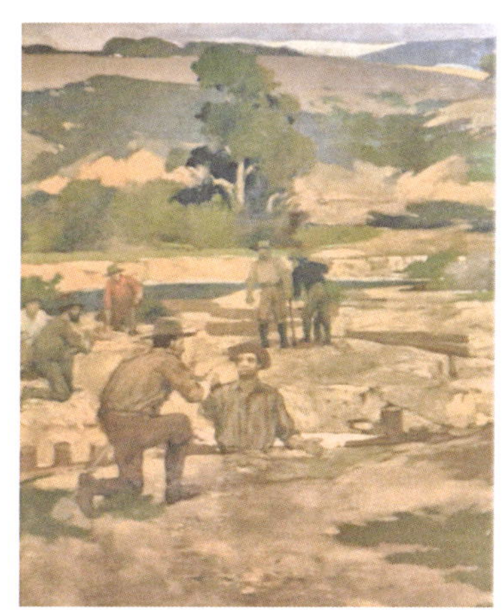

Artist Arthur F. Mathews' 12-painting mural originally hung on the first-floor rotunda, are now displayed on the lower level. The murals are an example of a regional artistic style known as "California Decorative." The work was commissioned in 1913, completed in 1915 in time for the Panama Pacific International Exposition. The paintings were moved from their original location during the 1976 restoration project.

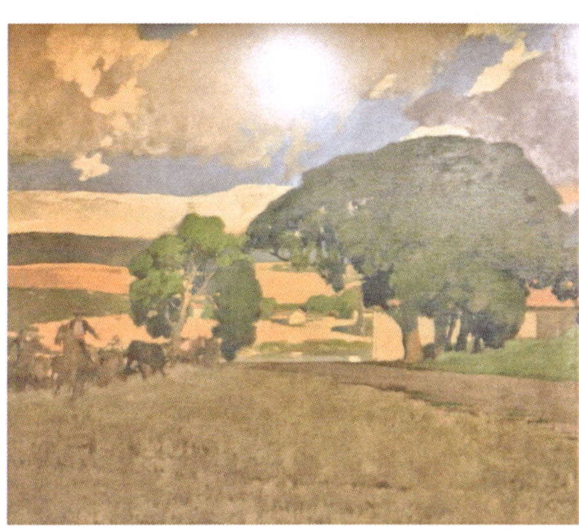
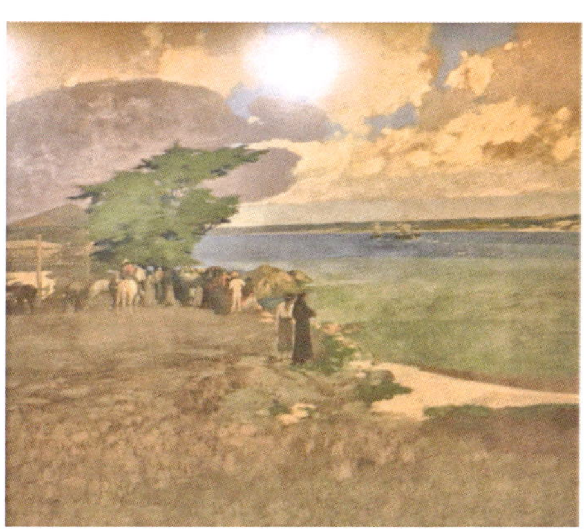
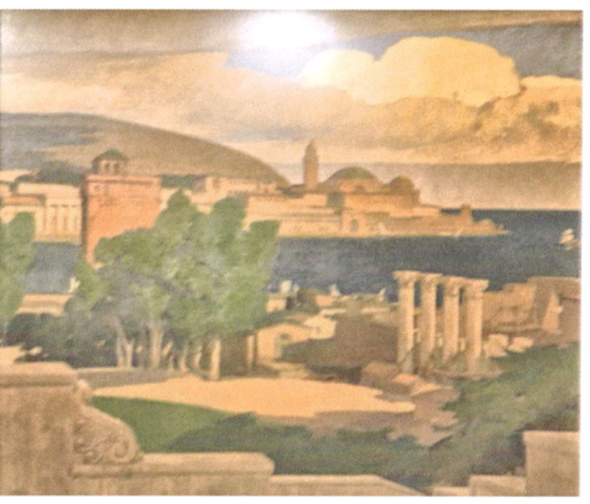

Art Deco

California's permanent capitol was constructed beginning in 1860 and completed in 1870.

Much of the interior design reflects that time period, including the brass doors of the elevator and the sconce lights in the legislative chambers' visitor gallery.

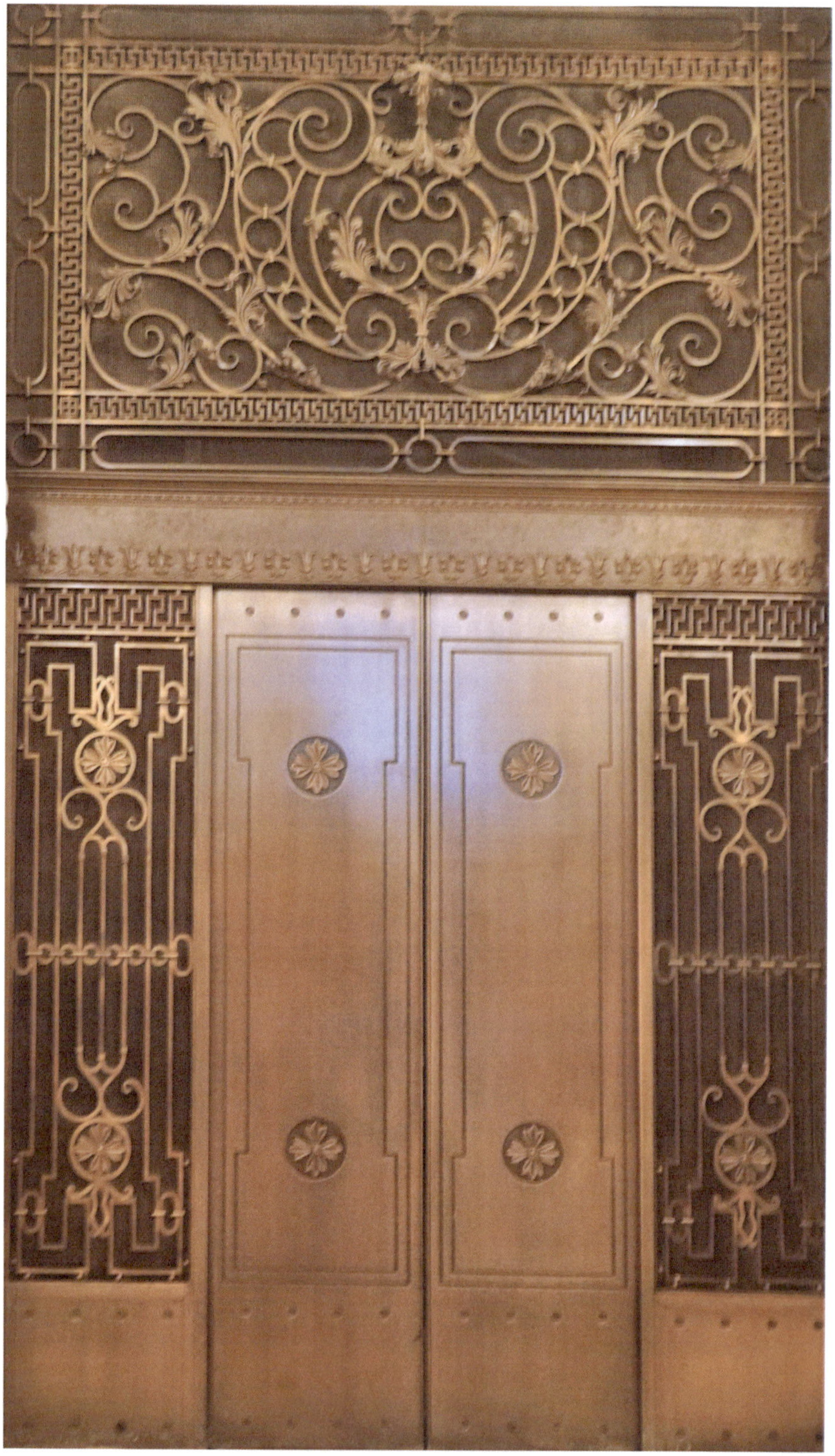

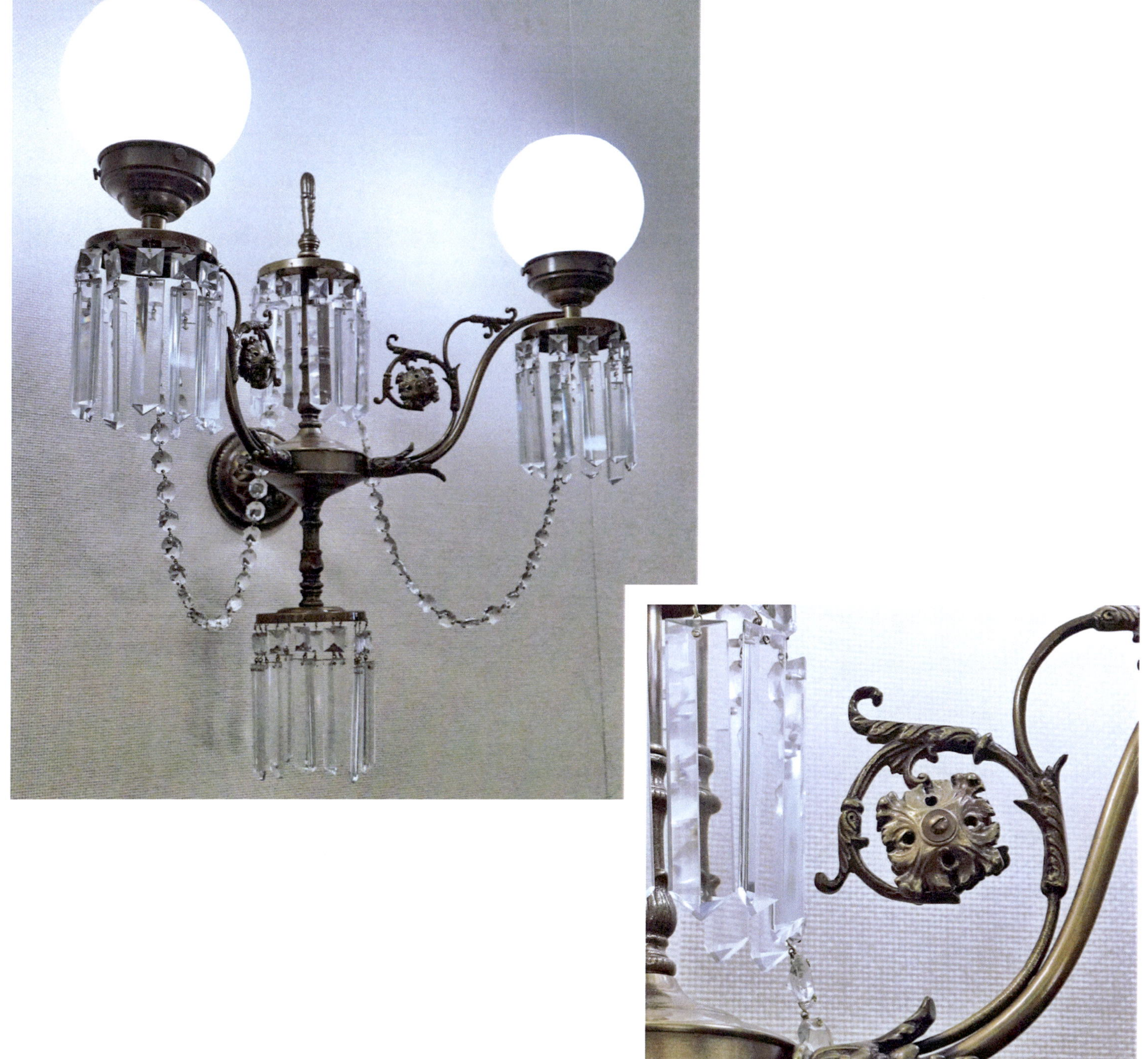

Eureka! California or Bust

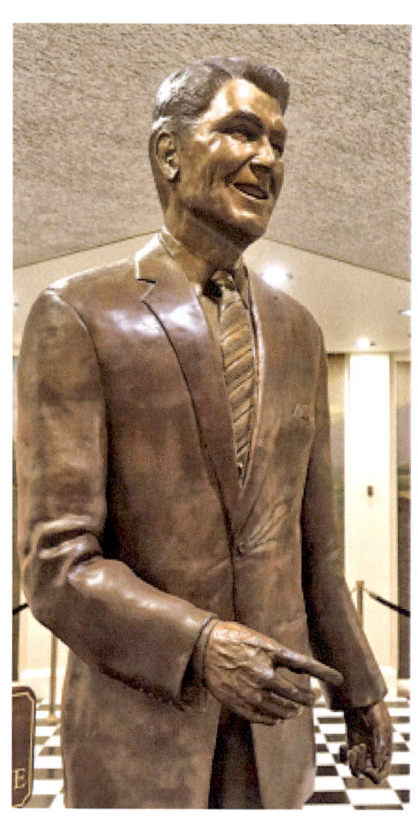

Upon reaching Sacramento I felt like a 49er in the Gold Rush. The use of gold in the capitol's inter or highlights the decorations elegan ly.

The first floor museum that displayed the original governor's office gives the visitor a look into the past. The tour guide gladly

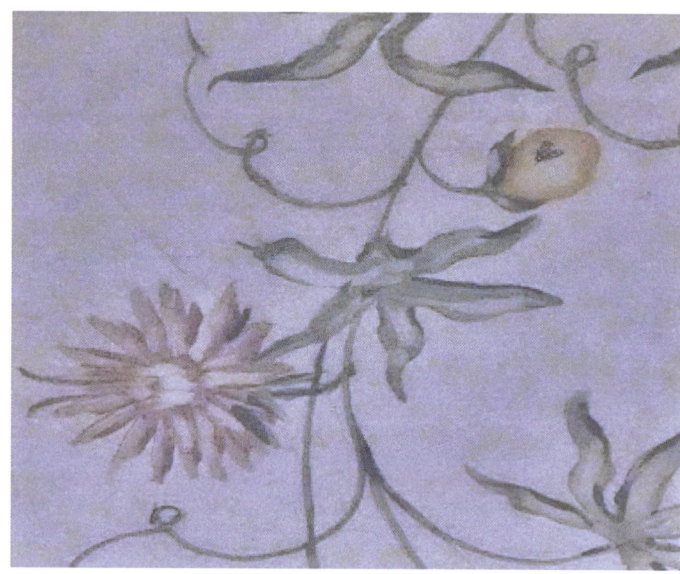

showed me the painted bee on the ceiling flower artwork acknowledging of the state's large agricultural production.

A life-size bronze statue of the late governor and United States President Ronald Reagan was a nice surprise in the lower level near the gift shop.

About the Photographer

Jane Moorman describes herself as an adventurer who loves to drive the backroads to see what there is to see.

During her 30-year journalism career, Jane honed her photographic skills as a photojournalist, including covering high school sporting events.

A friend once said, "I wish I could see the world as Jane sees it. Finding the beauty in things that most of us don't take time to see."

Upon retiring in 2021, Jane decided there is a lot of her native country she had not visited, including each state's capitol, so she began her journey of exploring the USA.

Jane currently lives in Albuquerque, New Mexico, but says her real home is on the road.

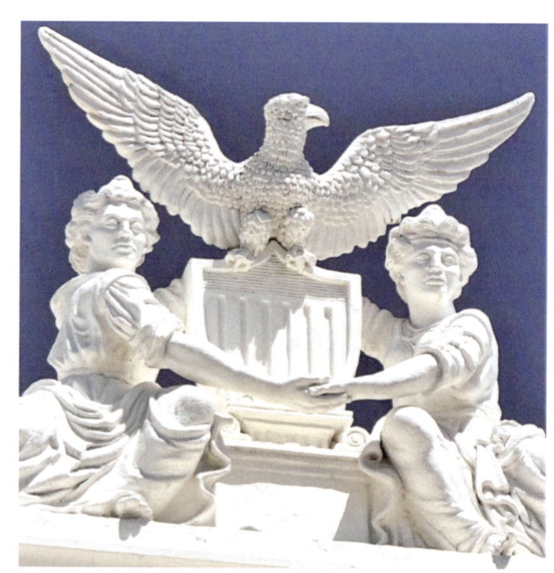